HINDSIGHT NOTWITHSTANDING

Hindsight Notwithstanding

Laura Zaino

Table Of Contents

Memory & Thought

Love, Hope, Love

Loss, aka Cancer Poems

Connection

Memory & Thought

1997, The Golden Dove Diner

Salt, pepper, sugar granules dusted across the
    gold-speckled formica.
The tiny puddle of a melting ice cube saturating the
    crumpled wrapper from a straw.
Lemon seeds on a saucer's edge.
Tears in the pink vinyl upholstery and cranky, aging
    springs.
That chip on the lip of the coffee cup, so smooth
    against your mouth.

The Difference Between

6:30 am,
I step out of the bathroom
into my mother's kitchen.
Her coffee crackles as it brews and
her groggy voice asks,
are you up early or late?
I can't sleep, I say.

There is freshly born light outside.
My mother stands at the window
looking towards a cloudless horizon.
The coffee must taste just like morning should,
refreshing as the air she breathes,
the air she steps into each day,
greeted by the sun.

Open Letter to 3 a.m.

I know you don't have many friends,
especially not on weekdays.

It's not your fault
people don't like to spend time with you
and they glare indignantly at your glowing digital lines,
so bright in their darkened rooms.
They are studying themselves, really.

Every night you creep in
dark and quiet ...
At first you seem so far away but
sure enough,
you always arrive.
You're dependable, at least.

3 a.m., you have youth on your side:
the promise of a new day,
the happy twenty-somethings who see you all the time.
You are moonlight.
You are stars.
You are dreams.
You're the bridge to tomorrow.
Maybe when we stare,
it's just because we're jealous.

winter haikus

dark lines of sleeping
trees draw stencils in the sky
above pure white ground

icicles flourish
gray clouds linger exactly
where they are meant to

first light

softening of darkness
gently the night sky withdraws
its earthly shroud

Reflections at the Bird Feeder

A bird alights to take some seed
and the world before me sings.
Imagine such ease in finding what you need!
A bird alights to take some seed.
It's lovely, yes, but I'll concede--
I'd rather hands than wings.
A bird alights to take some seed
and the world before me sings.

Filigree

You were wearing
a big blue coat
with big gold buttons down the middle.

I rode in the silver wagon
that pushed into my back but was perfect
for my fingers to hold onto.

And we walked through the aisles
of food and books and household items,
past refrigerators lining the perimeter.

I stopped to do my imaginary job
and stacked up the paper towels just right and neat,
then hid behind them on the shelf as always,
satisfied and cozy in my supermarket hideaway.
People passed and pretended not to notice me.

When my game was done your cart was gone;
your coat and your self and your hair
had left the paper towel and tissue aisle.

They weren't in the bread aisle either.
Your stirrup pants and light blue socks
weren't by soups, or cookies,
or along the great expanse of refrigerators.

No one had seen you with your big blue coat
and plain white sneakers.
No one had passed your goldish curls in a silver clip
over in aisle two.

I asked a man with a green vest a and name tag
who was piling eggs into the refrigerator.
"Are you lost?" he questioned.
"No," I declared,
"My mother is."

So he led me through those swinging doors
in the back of the store
that I had always peered past,
behind all the frozen goods—
a place I had always wondered about.

And I put my voice through a microphone.
"Come to the back of the store, "I told you,
in who know show many words,
replacing easy listening with comic relief
for tired shoppers.

You were wearing a big blue coat
with big gold buttons,
and I said "There she is"

as I spotted your laugh
coming around the bend.

The material was rough,
but blue's your favorite color,
and I'll never forget the design
carved into those buttons.

what really matters

the colors of hydrangeas
body language
moonrise
drinking enough water
moss on a massive gray stone alongside a hiking trail
the sound the screen door at my childhood home made
        as it closed
stop signs
the freckle on his right thumb
tree branches dancing in the wind
rhythm
the bucolic blue drawings on my grandmother's dishes
listening skills
heartfelt laughter
avocados

Tater Tots at the Grownup Table

Coexisting with superheroes
and weapons of mass destruction,
we dip each crispy mouthful into ketchup
one after another
until they are gone.
The children are spiraling;
they have no time for hunger.
We sit in the periphery,
drinks in hand,
and smile knowingly at each other.

After Dinner Thought

My fortune cookie told me yesterday:
"Keep on charging the enemy so long as there is life."
This is a surprising thing for a cookie to say, rather bold.
And, coming from a cookie,
it is both disconcerting and reassuring ...

What if the person before me or after me had
received this advice instead?
This tiny piece of paper could have been the
catalyst of a violent outrage,
a social revolution,
the full-fledged estrangement of a wary teenager.

There are people in the world
taking cues from things
even less appropriate than dessert.
It may be fortunate that these words fell to my eyes,
somewhat sane and more or less well-mannered. ...

This is good advice for me.
Not so much the "enemy" part, but the
"so long as there is life"
and the "keep on charging."
How different the whole idea becomes
when we eliminate the enemy altogether.

14

A Porn Star Falls In Love

There are at least
two sides to everything.
The dime gets spent,
head and tail.

Love, Hope, Love

i carry yr heart w/ me (i carry it in
my mind (my mind) my mind and the music
and the shadow of a doubt   i know
i know   i love you   and you love me
and i carry yr heart w/ me (i carry it in
my mind) (my mind) you can't get into)).
yr heart fits fine_ inside my mind_
w/ the love that i have for you . . .
but yr mind (yr mind) don't go w/ yr heart,
as hasn't it always, just always, been
<never did a mind follow a heart, a heart
follow a mind>   and so yr heart
lives (inside my mind) forever and you know it
and maybe i think maybe my mind lives
(within yr heart)   cause that's the piece
you love
not understanding

after e.e. cummings' poem
"[i carry your heart with me(i carry it in]"

Once Upon A Time

We know there is
neither reason nor excuse
we know these lips
should not know each other.
But I can taste you in my sleep
and I can make a dream come true
when we lie on your bed
and kiss.
And we kiss
and we kiss
and hands are happy,
body parts alert.
And we are terrible.

We know this
is going nowhere,
must end in frustration.
But you feel so good
and every moment only happens once
and youth is not here forever
and you feel so good
you make me smile all over.

Correspondence

I may have said before
that I'm not the type of person
who speaks with her hands.

One way or another
you may have told me before
you may have somehow
professed your love
but I never knew the language of it.
I only know the romance of it,
the way your syllables feel.

Perhaps the walls can fill me in later,
their would-be ears fluent in vibration,
their constant eyes open to your hands.

Until Summer

I wish every night was last Saturday night,
when the sleek glass vial of above-par cocaine
lasted five of us till nine in the morning
and we played pictionary on an eight-foot piece of paper
that was taped up on the wall.

Conversations made their ways around the room,
navigated people and subjects.
Music resonated in our voices.
Art bounced off the studio walls.
Ideas were almost visible and
the mirror that they dwelled in
traveled round, round, round.

And you, gentle and incomparable,
with such a soothing voice . . .
Between lines and
sips of dry red wine
you would tell me things.
We wore each other's earrings
and you played with my hair.

Later on, long after
the sun had risen for a Sunday,

the last of the linear bursts of mind
disappeared from our palate.

Our wits began to lose speed
but voices carried on excitedly.
There was a meaningful discussion about sex
and I looked over to your face,
past the lock of hair that fell right by your eyelashes
and danced and fluttered as you blinked your eyes.

near silence

the watch on his wrist
he wears through the night
so without glasses he can know the time

often we will stir from sleep
to readjust pillows and bodies
and after our heads find their places
there is quiet
and then
beep

the tiny blue light casts a glow
onto his face
he glances at the time
and rubs with two fingers
the bridge of his nose
right between those two eyes
that then turn to me

he is nearsighted
and I am
so close
to his body and spirit
so close to sleep

telephone

you responded
with the inconspicuous
same here
instead of the indulgent
I love you
and I grinned at the sincerity
in your delicate voice
I miss you
I said
and heard you smile

This Present Loving

We three are a maze
which I navigate slowly.
Even the straightaways are labyrinthine.
I mark each turn to map out later.

We three are my enigma.

One is dew forming on the grassblade,
one the dirt where it takes root.
I am that green and silver grass,
wavering in the breeze.

One is the leaf that rides the stream,
one the rock which current flows around.
My thirst is so great,
but I am the very water.

To My Ex-Lover

1. The Prison Dream

Two years, and you laid
unbothered in her arms
the day they took me away.
You hugged me so briefly,
asked not where or when
you might ever see me again.
I cried as I gave you, unsolicited,
a piece of paper
with the prison's name and address.
But you would never come,
that much was obvious.

2. Somewhere We Can Never Go

In dreams I see you all the time
and you seem indifferent, unkind,
though I know otherwise. I know
you, even in that world, will not open,
will not admit.
You are frightened of many things.
Remembering the occasional teardrops
you never wanted me to see,
I wonder at everyone, always so afraid.

This is what we are.
never hesitate to laugh, but refuse to cry.
This is what we are—
we cannot exist without water,
we do not exist without time.
You are not here and yet, time somehow passes.
I long for you in my dreams.

3. The Rescue Dream

Once while you slept:
There was a beach and I was drowning in the sea.
You ran to save me, but suddenly
jagged rocks stormed up from the ground,
running ahead of you,
blocking any path to the water.
Each step drove you further into the sand.

Cerulean

There was a sense of permanence with you,
a sort of blossom in the winter,
the cool, calm water under the ice.
I thought the lake was as deep as the Earth

but now there are seasons
that melt the surface,
and evaporation flies away
with our most beautiful crystals,
to dissipate
and pour down as rain.

Our smiles are scattered,
one love now a cloud,
the other somewhere a drop of ocean.

Sharing a Meal

I remember crying to myself in the Japanese restaurant,
hiding behind my hair and the noodle soup that required
        a lot of napkins.
But you noticed anyway, I'm sure.
You went to the bathroom and I distracted myself
with the discouraging task of using chopsticks for
        Udon noodles,
which kept splashing back into the bowl,
the soup jumping onto my face
and blending with the one or two tears I'd let go
while you were gone.
When you returned I manufactured an optimistic smile.

I remember crying to myself in the Japanese restaurant
and I remember your thoughtful silence,
the gentle gesture of offering spicy ginger sauce,
the unease in your generous eyes.

Driving Through Your Hometown

Streetlights cast their amber glow on the asphalt
and plentiful stars make this city girl swoon
though I never would have wanted to
grow up here, surrounded by such darkness,

the car's headlights never bright enough for me
to see around sharp corners of winding roads.
But now we smile as we search for
darker, darkest, place to stop this car and

make love, both outdoors and in, at once hiding
and in public, naked under stars and trees,
building memories that resemble
high school fantasy, ingredients key

for dreams I had when we first met, and I did
want you then, but our lives were on paths that we
never could have guessed would lead us here,
some road we somehow overlooked before.

I Am Hiding.

The more I love you
the softer your hair gets,
the smoother your kisses,
the wetter my lips.

The deeper I fall
toward love's glowing core
the less important all else seems.

I give in to this generous present
and I am saved from the past
as its wounds hide quietly
under their scars.

All I can do is inhabit you,
both my spider web and my cocoon.

Kin

Am I not the moon?
We are both made of the Earth,
one containing so much water
and the other
wanting water so much
it pulls the oceans
closer
day after day. Night after night
we greet each other.
The impenetrable expanse between us
is nothing but a giant pillow.
We rely on each other.
We are made of the same.
We dance in the light.

Loss, aka Cancer Poems

In Two Thousand Sixteen   *for J.W.*

There is no courage without fear.
There is no strength without adversity.
It is balance.
It is battle.
It is five hours every Thursday
when the regimented poison
delivers its fiery will into my veins.

Disease is not welcome here.
So I host righteous vigilante compounds,
expose my innocent blood to their extraordinary
fury,
microscopic yet supreme.
All shall burn;
evil and kind, grotesque and beautiful.
This is war
and chemotherapy is my front line.

Cancer is a worthy opponent.
But cancer lacks love.
Cancer lacks honor.
My chemical army is dispatched by humanity
and embodies compassion.
It is born from purpose and resolve.

Take the soft, peach-fuzzy hair.
Take my resistance to the common cold.
Pump me full of this ravenous, indiscriminate assault.
Give me life.

Love and Pain Must Coexist
               and That Must Be Beautiful

Ten days/two weeks later
we lie in her bed.
The house is almost empty,
almost cleared.
          Who would have wanted the antique jars?
          Who most needs a new computer?
We lie in her bed,
soft taupe sheets our Christmas gift the year before.
Constellation stickers on the ceiling still glow in
the dark,
twenty years after you jumped on the bed,
reaching up with little boy arms.
          Who will find the memories left in her
          dresser drawer?
          Who will sit out on the porch to watch the
          river drift by?

I caress you softly as you travel the tightrope
          toward sleep,
an act full of valor and unpredictability.
Tonight you fall
into yourself, into memories and projections.
You cry out and I hold you, you sob and
          my body aches.

The affairs are in order,
the house almost cleared.
But who can replace the gentle hand of a
mother?

Prologue

One of his last confrontations with death
was different from all the others.
He saw its pupils widening,
felt the persuasive warmth of its grasp.

We gathered around his trembling body
and mustered little bundles of bravery,
wisdom, and relief.
We held his weathered hands
and hugged his tired body.
We told him easeful things
as tears rushed down our faces
and flushed our skin.

Hours later, he awoke,
despite this ultimate surrender.
The gesture alone had satisfied death
for the time being.

Pictures of Donnie Schoonmaker

Sometime in the mid 80s: you stand on a giant
          boulder/ tiny mountain,
arms outstretched, your auburn perm crazed with
          humidity.
Your young son stands with you, beaming.
Joy cascades down to the camera.

Late 90s--yet another party in your kitchen,
another smile (always a smile) on your face.
You wear an eyepatch and a gold earring, arms
          around friends.
Your teenage son is all teeth, skin, and jawline
          in his toga.

2000s. You and me and your son,
all laughing, for no reason I can imagine
other than clear weather and warm hearts.
We all wear baseball hats
as we sit on the back bumper of your van,
holding each other close.
Here yours is a toothless grin;
the recurring cancer war has claimed its first
          casualties.

In the 2010s you are much smaller, with a
        mustache to match.
You hold your grandson on your lap,
that giant joyous countenance only a one year old
        can manage.
He's looking out past the camera as you bounce him,
platinum hair flopping around.
His vibrancy complements your wide gummy grin.

As time continues to pass, my memories of you become
        snapshots.
It's been years since I spoke to you,
since anyone has spoken to you,
laughed with you,
listened to music with you.

I can still hear your laugh--
a little high pitched, a little raspy.
I can still see you tapping your dry workhorse fingers
on the plastic coated tablecloth,
following the beat,
stopping to get up from the table
and move on to the next thing.

Connection

Yet
(spring 2021, a year into the Covid pandemic)

There shall be no undoing.
There shall be no giving up, no letting down.
No stepping back, no turning away.
Every morning we rise to face another day,
its ferocity yet unyielding.

What is it about resilience that keeps us coming back?
Even the word itself is hard to grasp,
slithery sounding, it sneaks away.
But we re-visit, re-establish, re-try, re-peat.
The days get longer.
We see the smile hiding in the sun.

Resilience holds silence:
the good, the best kind of silence.
The kind you need,
the kind that pulls you through the noise and madness
to the beautiful side of spring,
that breaks through dark and frozen soil
towards the light again.

Resist the persistent darkness,
eyes open wide.
Re-Silence.
Breathe.
Resilience.   47

Recommended Behaviors For An Interesting Life

If you must carry an umbrella,
only do so when the sky is clear, never under rain.
Gotta keep that atmosphere guessing.
Don't let it know it has the upper hand.
Proclaim emphatically,
"There are things I know that you do not!"
as you shake your fist at the sky.

Memorize random miscellaneous facts.
(A cheetah's top speed is an estimated 75 miles
            an hour.
Its gestation period is between 90 and 98 days.)
When morning comes
remember that it is morning only because we have
            deemed it so,
that the sun and its planets have already been
            dancing forever,
regardless of what takes place on or within them.
Sunrise and sunset have no idea they exist.
The circumstances on which our lives are based
are merely side effects
            of absurdly magnificent events.

(It takes approximately 8 minutes and 20 seconds
for sunlight to reach Earth.)

Switch hands.
Keep your brain on its toes.
Strong feet make decisive movements,
which cultivates strength
and humbles the rambunctious ego.

Maintain passive interests.
You'll learn about other planes on which you coexist,
catch glimpses into tents in the forest
and at the undersides of cars.
You'll add to your arsenal of miscellaneous facts
as you repeatedly remind yourself how to
pronounce oenology.

Finally,
understand there are 24 hours in each day, not 12,
and refer to them accordingly.
Bedtime under a darkened sky
should not share name or number
with morning, or midday, or lunch;
it is far more poignant.
You dream some dreams
and nourish your subconscious
as planets float blithely on.
Your clock counts hours,

maintains some state of affairs
concerning the collective consciousness.

(All units of time are based on and can be reduced
to measures of distance.)

Offering

In the winter of my life
I hope there is snow in decided abundance
so that I might make myself a great snowwoman
who shall melt back into the earth
with the coming of spring
to nourish the burgeoning ground.

Crossroad of Birthright and Logic

Sometimes you can see where the rain stops.
You'll notice the sidewalk darkening across the street
while your side remains dry and pale.
Whenever I find myself in this rare moment I am at
          first awestruck,
but quickly remind myself that the rain has to stop
          somewhere, after all,
and in doing so dispel that effervescent wonder,
that beauty we have all so earnestly been seeking
since its slow and deliberate evaporation sometime
          early on.

Lens

You carry firewood and clear weeds.
You consider planting trees and laying stones.
I move around the house gazing through windows,
thinking how one day I'll clean them.
I imagine myself as part of the world.
I observe potential
and keep gazing.

Mirror, Mirror, Everywhere

Objects in mirror are closer
then
they appear.
The rear view magnifies
what first only on the horizon lies.

Navigation

We take our medicine carefully.
We dole it out one measured dose at a time,
ever mindful of the side effects,
the after effects,
the longing.

> 400 mg ibuprofen
> .25 mg xanax
> 2 oz whiskey
> 15 mg adderall

When I step out onto the sidewalk
I look up at the sky,
trying to reason with the moon.
"I thought you were supposed to have answers," I say.
"Especially with me being a woman and all."
I negotiate with nature,
discuss the terms of my engagement.
"I live symbiotically," I argue.
"I give and I take, and I *give*."

There will always be something else.
Something more, or less, or different.

The dosage feels weaker.
We reassess, readjust.

We take our medicine carefully.
We are ever mindful of its side effects,
its risks.

    3 pints beer
    3 shots espresso
    1 joint marijuana

I close my eyes and step into myself.
There will always be something else, more or less.
I step into myself and
I visit the Source.
"It will all be fine," she says.
"Everything is in order. It is divine," he says.
The Source sends me along.
There are stars in the sky and plants in the ground.
Everything is as it should be.

I follow the sidewalk back to my door.
The road to home is long.

Break Glass In Case Of Emergency

Climb out the window onto the fire escape.
Be careful of any weak, rusted metal under your feet
as you descend the side of the building.
It is important to use extreme caution -- though
        this is an escape route,
with every step you risk falling to uncertainty.
At the end of your climb there will be a great leap involved,
the final measure necessary in bringing yourself to
        the ground.

Once you have reached the earth,
do not attempt to forget what was inside that window
on the third, the fifth, the tenth floor.
All we leave behind still lives a little somewhere
        inside us,
and every so often you will need to distill some
        fervid memory
or extinguish an ember
or even just let it engulf you,
if only for a moment or two.

Trick Question

Let Life Be Simple.
What have you got to lose?

Made in the USA
Middletown, DE
03 March 2022